KALEIDOSCOPE* DUETS BOOK 5

by Jon George

FOREWORD

The KALEIDOSCOPE Duet Books one through five correspond in all respects to the KALEIDOSCOPE Solo Books one through five, and are intended for simultaneous use.

These duets have been designed to provide students with the invaluable experience of ensemble performance from their earliest studies: the lessons to be learned in co-operative effort, in more objective listening, in rhythmic precision, will be appreciated by every teacher.

The secondo parts are no more difficult than the primo parts, so that each student may become familiar with both parts; the insight and confidence gained in this manner have no substitute, and will prove to have a special value to students preparing for public performance.

TABLE OF CONTENTS

D1275168

*Kaleidoscope (kə-līdə-skōp), n. 1. A tubelike instrument containing loose bits of colored glass reflected by internal mirrors so that various symmetrical patterns appear as the instrument is rotated. 2. **Anything that constantly changes, as in color and design.**

THIS WIDE LAND

secondo

Triumphantly!

JON GEORGE

THIS WIDE LAND

primo

Triumphantly!

JON GEORGE

THE BROOK

secondo

JON GEORGE

THE BROOK
primo

JON GEORGE

THE BELLS OF ST. GERVAIS
secondo

JON GEORGE

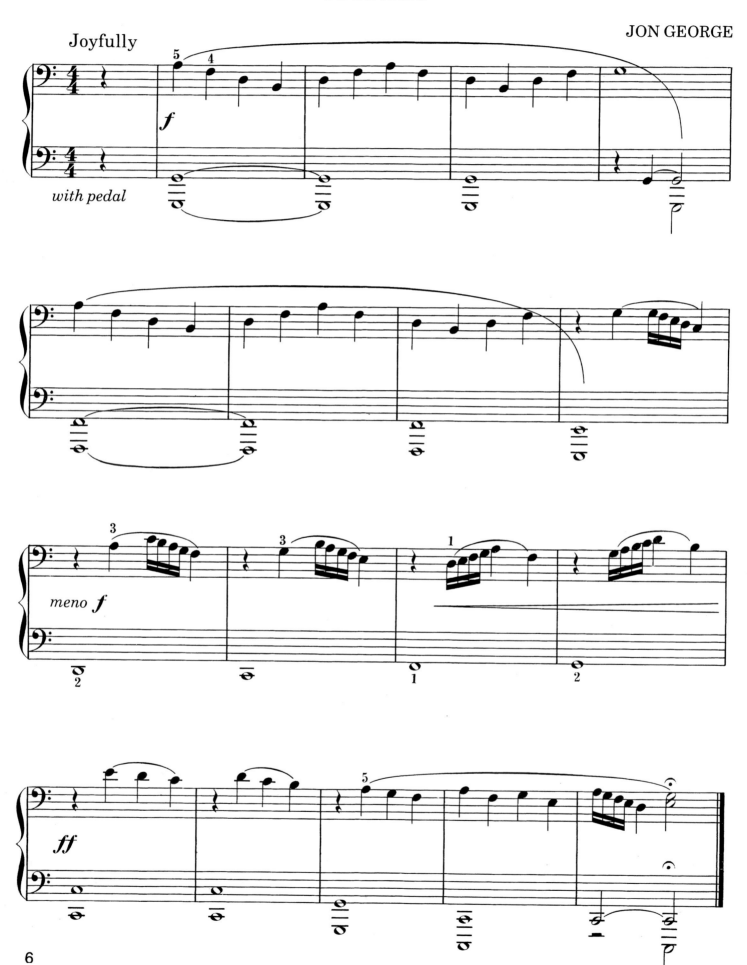

THE BELLS OF ST. GERVAIS

primo

JON GEORGE

MELODY

secondo

With firm but pleasant tone

JON GEORGE

MELODY

With firm but pleasant tone

JON GEORGE

FACTORY SCENE

secondo

JON GEORGE

Industriously

10

FACTORY SCENE

primo

JON GEORGE

ENCHANTED FOREST

secondo

Ethereally

JON GEORGE

12

ENCHANTED FOREST
primo

JON GEORGE

Ethereally

* Pedal marking for solo performance

MOUVEMENT ÉNERGIQUE

secondo

JON GEORGE

MOUVEMENT ÉNERGIQUE

primo

JON GEORGE

Moving quickly